AUSTRALIA IN HISTORY

Gallipoli and the Middle East, 1915-18

A.K. Macdougall

Waverton Press

Waverton Press
Level 1
100 Bay Road
Waverton NSW 2060
Australia
Email: publishing@fivemile.com.au

First published 2004
All rights reserved
© The Five Mile Press

Edited by Samone Bos
Designed by Sylvia Witte

Printed in China

National Library of Australia Cataloguing-in-Publication data
Macdougall, Anthony, 1943– .
Gallipoli and the Middle East.
Includes index.
For lower to middle secondary students.

ISBN 1 74124 088 3.

1. World War, 1914–1918 – Campaigns – Turkey – Gallipoli Peninsula – Juvenile literature. I. Title. (Series: Australia in History).

940.426

The photographs in this book came from the author's archives.

The following photographs are reproduced courtesy of the Australian War Memorial, Canberra: Page 6 (AWM photo A3272); page 7 and cover (top 2nd from right) (AWM photo A3351); page 9 (AWM photo G549); page 10 and cover (top 2nd from left) (AWM photo A1829); page 12 (AWM photo G1810B); page 13 (AWM photo G635); page 14 (AWM photo G408); page 18 (AWM photo G309); page 19 and cover (bottom right) (AWM photo G3614); page 20 (AWM photo B1439); page 21 (AWM photo B1414); pages 24 and 25 and cover (2nd from bottom right) (colour photographs in AWM Collection by Captain Frank Hurley, AIF); page 27 (AWM photo B79); page 28 (AWM photo B300).

Every attempt has been made to trace and acknowledge copyright. Where an attempt has been unsuccessful, the publisher would be pleased to hear from the copyright owner so any omission or error can be rectified.

Contents

The Dardanelles and Gallipoli: The background	4
1914: The outbreak of war	6
The build-up to Gallipoli	8
Gallipoli: The invasion	10
Gallipoli: The crucial first day	12
Gallipoli: 'Digging in'	14
Gallipoli: Stalemate	16
Gallipoli: The campaign fails	18
Egypt, Iraq and oil	20
From Egypt to Palestine	22
Advancing to Jerusalem	24
Syria: Galloping to victory	26
The Middle East: Picking up the pieces	28
The making of the modern Middle East	30
Glossary	32
Index	32

The Dardanelles and Gallipoli: The background

Since recorded history began, the narrow stretch of water separating Asia from Europe – the Dardanelles – has been a focus of rivalries and a scene of wars. The ancient Greeks called the waters between Gallipoli and the Asian shore the 'Hellespont' because in ancient legend the heroine Helle had drowned there. The Hellespont connected the Mediterranean and the Aegean seas to the riches of the Black Sea. Greek legends also spoke of a mighty city on the Asian shore overlooking the southern entrance to the Straits called Ilium – Troy. The Greek states had besieged Troy more than 600 BC, a saga that inspired the great epic poems *The Iliad* and *The Odyssey*. Near the northern neck of the Straits, the Greeks founded a colony that grew into one of the most powerful cities of the known world – Byzantium.

In time, Byzantium became Constantinople, the fabled capital of the Eastern Roman Empire and seat of the Eastern (Orthodox) Christian Church. Its fall to the Ottoman Turks in 1453 was shattering to the kingdoms of Europe. The Turkish armies had conquered most of the Balkan peninsula a century earlier, defeating the Serbs at Kosovo as early as 1389. Turkish power remained a threat until 1689, when their armies reached the walls of Vienna itself. Then the Turkish tide receded. A new power, imperial Russia, threatened Turkey's Balkan realms. Russia's fleet and trading ships remained bottled up in the Black Sea unless she could seize from Turkey the neck of the bottle – Constantinople and the Dardanelles.

Britain and France shared Turkey's fear of Russian expansion and twice came to Turkey's aid when Russian armies marched into the Balkans to seize Constantinople. In 1854, Britain and France landed an army on the Gallipoli peninsula before shipping it to the Crimea on the Black Sea to destroy Russia's naval base at Sevastopol. In 1878, they used threats and diplomacy to force Russian armies to withdraw from the walls of Constantinople, while also making Turkey grant a form of independence to the Balkan states of Romania, Serbia and Bulgaria. The terms of the Congress of Berlin (1878) were humiliating to both Russia and Turkey because even Austria-Hungary shared in the spoils. Austria-Hungary could occupy (but not annex) the Turkish province of Bosnia-Herzegovina. For a thousand years, Slavs (Serbs and Croats) had lived in the province side by side with Muslims. It was a region of bitterness and hatred.

Two armed camps

By the early years of the 20th century, the balance of power in Europe had changed. In the 1890s, the new empire of Germany and the old empire of Austria-Hungary were

In 1914, the red flag of Turkey flew over an empire that stretched from Egypt to the Balkans and Arabia.

Australia in History

allied against Russia and France. Great Britain, which had kept free of any European alliances since Napoleon's time, was so alarmed by Germany's growing naval and commercial power that she signed a friendship pact with France (the *Entente Cordiale*) in 1904 and another friendship pact with Russia in 1907. Europe had now drifted into two armed camps.

The Great Powers regarded the declining empire of Turkey as not worth an alliance. But the 'Sick Man of Europe', as Turkey was called, was soon to come back to life.

By 1914, Turkey's fears of Austria and Russia had led her to forge closer ties with Germany, which sent General von Sanders to Constantinople to reform the Turkish Army.

The 'Young Turk' revolution, 1908

In July 1908, the long and murderous rule of Turkey's Sultan Abdul Hamid came to a sudden end. A small group of young Turkish Army officers led a mutiny in Salonika. The rest of the Sultan's army joined them in their demand for reform. The 'Young Turks' promised elections and enthroned a new Sultan, pledging increased autonomy for the empire's subject races. This radical new policy alarmed both Austria and Russia.

Two months later, Russia's foreign minister Isvolsky, confident of the support of both Britain and France, met with Austria-Hungary's foreign minister Baron Aerenthal, and made an extraordinary proposal. If Austria agreed to Russia getting a revision of the 1878 treaty forbidding Russia's fleet from passing through the Dardanelles, Russia would agree to Austria annexing outright Bosnia-Herzegovina. Serbia would be inflamed at seeing Bosnia's Serb inhabitants pass permanently under Austrian rule, but Russia was now hopeful of gaining Constantinople.

Bosnia annexed, 1908

But Austria outfoxed Russia. On 5 October 1908, Austria announced that Bosnia-Herzegovina were now part of her empire – annexed. Russia, her deceit exposed, was forced to accept the fact. Serbia mobilised her small but tough army for war against Austria, but was without allies. Instead, the Serbs began a terrorist campaign against the Austrian administrators of Bosnia. Austria decided to eliminate Serbia completely at the first opportunity. The chance came in 1914.

Turkey's empire suffered further loss. In 1911, Italy seized Libya from the Turks. In October 1912, the Balkan nations of Serbia, Bulgaria, Montenegro and Greece, with Russia's encouragement, drove Turkey's armies from the Balkans, leaving Turkey in 1913 with just the land around Constantinople – and the Gallipoli peninsula.

Gallipoli and the Middle East, 1915–18

1914: The outbreak of war

When Bosnian Serb fanatics assassinated the heir to the throne of Austria-Hungary in Sarajevo in June 1914, few people thought that soon all the Great Powers of Europe would be at war. But on 28 July, Austria-Hungary, confident of a quick victory, declared war on Serbia. Russia mobilised for war. Germany declared war on Russia on 1 August and then France. On 4 August, German armies invaded neutral Belgium to outflank the French armies and as a result Britain declared war on Germany. When news of this was received early on 5 August, Australia – as part of the British Empire – was also at war.

In Australia and New Zealand, thousands of men volunteered to serve in the army being raised to assist Britain. All hoped they would soon be in Belgium or France, where British and French armies were fighting the invading Germans. Everyone thought that the war would be 'over by Christmas' and that the Allied armies would soon be marching on Berlin and Vienna. Few thought that the 'Great European War' would last four years, resulting in the death of eight million soldiers.

The AIF is born

A great volunteer force of 20,000 Australians was formed into the '1st Australian Division' – consisting of three infantry brigades and a brigade of artillery. A brigade of Light Horse was soon added, and there were so many volunteers that more units were formed. Their commander Major-General William Throsby Bridges decided early that the Australian troops would form their own army, fighting together under their own officers, and would not be split up to serve in British units. They would form the 'Australian Imperial Force' – its initials (AIF) soon became famous throughout the world.

A great convoy of 26 ships carrying the Australians and the 10 transports bearing the New Zealand Expeditionary Force (NZEF) steamed for Egypt from Western Australia on 1 November 1914, escorted by British, Australian

Young Australians volunteered for the army in their thousands. These troops sailing to seize German New Guinea later served on Gallipoli.

Australia in History

and Japanese warships. They were passing the Cocos Islands when the German cruiser *Emden* was sighted there. HMAS *Sydney* sped west to Cocos at full steam and destroyed *Emden* after a 25-minute battle. As the convoy was proceeding to Egypt, news came that Turkey had joined Germany in the war against Britain, France and Russia.

A new enemy: Turkey

In 1914, all the Great Powers had hoped that Turkey would remain neutral. The Sultan's empire was weak, his army exhausted by its defeats since 1911. The Young Turk officers who ruled in the Sultan's name had encouraged Germany to provide military and financial assistance to their ailing country. Germans were building the railway to Baghdad, but British officers were training Turkey's navy. Some Young Turk officers like Colonel Mustafa Kemal distrusted all foreign alliances, but hoped that the empire would adopt European ways. Turkey's fate, however, was in the hands of the charismatic but ruthless Enver Pasha.

Enver was eager to share in the defeat of Russia, and on 2 August 1914 signed a secret alliance with Germany. Two days later, the German warships *Goeben* and *Breslau* steamed from the Adriatic for Constantinople. Turkey allowed them to enter the Dardanelles – despite international treaty – and anchor off Constantinople. In September 1914, Enver ordered minefields to be laid in the Dardanelles, effectively closing the Straits to all shipping except his own. In one stroke, most of Russia's seaborne trade was cut off. Russia now could neither export her wheat and oil nor import the **munitions** she needed. On 29 October, the two German warships bombarded Russian naval bases in the Black Sea and a week later Britain, France and Russia declared war.

When Turkey entered the war in 1914, its Sultan, who was also the religious leader of his Islamic subjects, called for a *jihad* – a Holy War to defend Islam. Few Muslims followed his call. Most of his subjects were Sunni Muslims, a tolerant sect, and 25 per cent of his people were Jews or Christians (Slavs, Greeks and Armenians), who had long been allowed to practice their religions. Even the Arabs and Kurds, who were Muslim, were eager to break free from Turkish rule.

Swift and ruthless in crushing rebellions, the Turkish Empire was tolerant in matters of religion. But it was inefficient and backward. Telephone lines, merchant shipping, automobiles and railways were almost non-existent. The empire moved at the pace of its camel caravans. The Middle East nations familiar to us nowadays were unknown. The Arab lands between Egypt and Anatolia were known simply as Greater Syria, and were split up into numerous small *vilayets* (provinces) such as those of Jerusalem and Damascus. The ancient region now known as Iraq, which Europeans then called 'Mesopotamia' – 'between the rivers' – was made up of three provinces of differing Islamic sects – Shia (Shi'ite), Sunni and Kurd.

An Australian soldier in the khaki uniform and bush hat (slouch hat) adopted for the troops enlisted for overseas service in the Australian Imperial Force.

Gallipoli and the Middle East, 1915–18

The build-up to Gallipoli

Egypt

The 30,000 Australians and New Zealanders arriving in Egypt in December 1914 became part of the **garrison** there defending the Suez Canal. Britain had declared a '**protectorate**' over Egypt and a disorganised Turkish attempt to cross the Canal was easily repulsed early in 1915. It seemed proof that the Turks were poor fighters.

The 'Australian and New Zealand Army Corps', which now consisted of two divisions, was placed under the command of an English lieutenant-general, Sir William Birdwood. The Australians soon got to like 'Birdie'. He was slight of build, without snobbery, and gifted with a sense of humour. He was amused by the Australians' down-to-earth nature, but disturbed that so few of them bothered to salute him.

The Australians were bored training in the deserts of Egypt while the real war was being fought in Europe, and many of them created a bad impression on the British and the Egyptians. On leave in Cairo, some Australians took over tram-cars and drove them at speed and others stole fruit from vendors. Many soldiers broke out of camp at night to have fun in Cairo. Australians found these antics highly amusing, but British senior officers described the Australians as a rabble, lacking the fine discipline of the British soldier. Others who knew the Australians' independent nature felt sure they would prove good soldiers because they were not only physically tough but full of spirit.

In his book *Gallipoli*, published in 1916, the English writer John Masefield, a future Poet Laureate of England, described the Australian and New Zealand soldiers in Egypt as '… *the finest body of young men ever brought together in modern times. For sheer physical beauty and nobility of bearing they surpassed any men I have ever seen.*' Another Englishman, Admiral Wemyss, RN, wrote in a letter in March: '*The Australians are the most magnificent body of men I have ever seen. I thought the Canadians splendid raw material, but these men are even finer. They are wild of course, but such pleasant looking fellows.*'

Anzac is born

At this time, a stores officer at headquarters suggested that the Corps' cumbersome name be shortened to the initials 'A.N.Z.A.C.' to make paperwork easier. The word quickly caught on and Birdwood decided it would be the official code-name for the Corps. Soon all Australians and New Zealanders serving overseas would be called 'Anzacs'.

The Dardanelles plan

In the cold, snow-bound winter at the end of 1914, Allied leaders were faced by deadlock on both the Western and Eastern fronts. The German armies had been stopped before they reached Paris, but so had the Russian armies marching on Berlin, and they were now facing their enemies in the snows of Poland after suffering enormous losses. Allied leaders wondered how they could break the **stalemate**.

In December 1914, the War Cabinet in London had discussed the opening of a new battlefront in the Mediterranean, perhaps against

Australia in History

Turkey. In early January 1915, the Russian high command asked the British government to mount some sort of 'demonstration' to deflect Turkish forces from its armies in the Caucasus. Eleven days later, Winston Churchill, the dynamic 40-year-old minister for the Royal Navy (First Lord of the Admiralty), enthralled the War Cabinet with a bold plan to mount a naval attack on the Dardanelles. Churchill suggested that a fleet of old battleships steam through the Dardanelles, pounding the forts on the Gallipoli peninsula with their massive guns, and then occupy Constantinople, the heart of Turkey's empire. If the attacks were successful, the wavering Balkan states could be won over to the Allied cause, and a Balkan front established to aid Russia.

Two days later on 15 January 1915, the Cabinet authorised the operation. The British Fleet began a month-long bombardment of the southern tip of Gallipoli, while a great army was gathered in Egypt. Birdwood was informed that his 30,000 Anzac troops might be used if a military force was also needed to land on Gallipoli itself.

The naval attacks

A great fleet of 18 British and French battleships steamed into the Dardanelles on the clear spring morning of 18 March 1915, bombarding the shore forts as they headed towards 'The Narrows', preceded by minesweepers. The Turkish forts soon ran out of ammunition and panic broke out in the capital. Suddenly, the French battleship *Bouvet* exploded and sank in minutes with 600 of her sailors. Two British battleships then hit mines and began to sink and three others were damaged. The fleet retired, beaten.

Above: Early in 1915 a great invasion armada began gathering for the Dardanelles campaign.

Gallipoli and the Middle East, 1915–18

Gallipoli: The invasion

Four days after the Allied navy's failure, the British Admiral told his generals that the fleet could not make another attempt without help from the army. General Sir Ian Hamilton, the Commander-in-Chief of the 'Mediterranean Expeditionary Force' (as the army gathering in Egypt was called) ordered plans drawn up for landings on the Gallipoli peninsula to take place in a month's time. There were so many delays that the invasion date was postponed another week – it would now take place on Sunday 25 April 1915. Churchill was appalled when he heard that the naval attack had been discontinued and the campaign had become a land *offensive* cobbled together in a hurry. He was unfairly blamed for the Gallipoli disaster for the rest of his long life.

Hamilton resolved to land his veteran British troops (tough, well-trained regulars of the 29th Division) at Cape Helles at the southern tip of Gallipoli, at no fewer than six beaches, while his other British formation, the under-trained Royal Naval Division, distracted the Turks by pretending to land in the north of the peninsula. The small French army would land near the ruins of ancient Troy as a diversion. This left the two Anzac divisions, which the British gave the 'easy task' of landing up the coast from Cape Helles, near the Gaba Tepe headland. From there, the Anzacs could strike east across the peninsula and cut off the Turks retreating from the south. Hamilton anticipated only 3,000 casualties and planned to march into Constantinople in two or three weeks. Medical services, ammunition and reserves were stockpiled for a 'short campaign'.

Australian troops assemble on the deck of a British warship on the way to Gallipoli. Note that they are wearing British peaked caps; they later discarded them and resumed wearing their slouch hats.

Australia in History

Thus was born the Gallipoli expedition. Like so many campaigns urged by political leaders and organised too hastily and with inadequate forces, it would depend in the end on the sheer bravery of the common soldiers to rescue it from disaster.

The landing at Anzac Cove, 25 April 1915

The Australians were the first Allied troops to land on the Gallipoli peninsula. General Birdwood chose the 3rd Brigade to carry out the first dawn landings because most of its 4,000 men were tough, practical bushmen who would not be easily fazed by difficulties. Their officers had told them that they must advance as far inland as the 'Third Ridge', and secure the rugged terrain. The 'Main Force', landing to their south near Gaba Tepe headland, could then strike inland over easy country.

Before dawn on Sunday 25 April 1915, the three battleships carrying the first wave of Australians had reached the coast near Gaba Tepe headland. The troops began clambering quietly into the rowing boats that would be towed in groups to the beaches by small steamboats. The sea was still, like glass, as the steamboats chugged towards the shore. It was pitch dark because the moon had set at 3 a.m. and the sun was yet to rise. But then things started going wrong. It seems that some of the leading steamers mistook the small headland of Ari Burnu for the promontory of Gaba Tepe; others maintain that a strong northerly current carried the boats off course. All agree that the first boats grounded on the shingle at 4.30 a.m., and that Turkish bullets suddenly began hitting the Australians.

The Australians found themselves on a narrow stretch of sand below high and sloping cliffs. 'Something clearly was wrong,' the Australian Official Historian later wrote. 'Everything seemed wrong.'

It is said that the Anzac fighting man was born at that moment. The Australians fixed their bayonets and calmly began to climb the steep slope, clawing at tussocks to steady themselves, and drove off the few Turks they found. As dawn broke, the troops reaching the summit of the cliffs saw before them a nightmare terrain of scrub-covered hills, ridges, gullies and ravines. They had been landed at the base of the Sari Bair Range itself, more than two kilometres off course. The terrible terrain was destined to be their battlefield for the next eight months.

The second wave of Australians landed at a small beach just south of Ari Burnu headland – the beach later known as Anzac Cove – from where several dry gullies led inland. The British Navy continued to land the rest of the 1st Australian Division at Anzac Cove, but soon their transports laden with troops came under Turkish shellfire. In the afternoon, the New Zealand Brigade was landed and pushed up to defend the ridges north of the beach, where enemy counter-attacks were mounting in intensity.

General Sir Ian Hamilton, a hero of the Boer War, was appointed to command the Allied army invading Gallipoli.

Gallipoli and the Middle East, 1915–18

Gallipoli: The crucial first day

The day of the landing saw some of the most terrible fighting of the Gallipoli campaign. When their officers fell to Turkish bullets, small parties of Australians pushed inland, and fought and died where they stood. Some men reached Third Ridge and others climbed the summit of the height called 'Baby 700'. They were overwhelmed by Turkish attacks because at about 10 a.m. the enemy began counter-attacking in strength. In the south, the Australians were clinging to the high area of flat terrain known as '400 Plateau', where a lonely pine-tree stood, but here also torrents of shellfire had halted their advance.

The Australians at Anzac Cove had the misfortune of facing troops commanded by the most dynamic Turkish commander of the war – a 34-year-old Albanian officer named Mustafa Kemal, who is known to history as Kemal Atatürk, father of the modern Turkish Republic. When Kemal was awoken at his headquarters with news that 'the English' had landed near Gaba Tepe, he immediately mounted his horse and led his 57th Regiment to the scene. By nightfall, Kemal's three regiments had thrown the Australians off Baby 700, and the Anzacs were barely clinging to the seaward edge of 400 Plateau, their last grip on Second Ridge.

Below: The Gallipoli battlefield. This is the terrible terrain that greeted the Australians after they climbed the cliffs at Anzac Cove.

Australia in History

Above: English officers remarked that on Gallipoli the Australians charged into battle like a football scrum.

By the end of the 'first day of Anzac' the Australians were holding the ragged crests of First Ridge, digging trenches to await the inevitable counter-attacks, while the air sang with the whine and crack of bullets, machine-gun fire and shells. They thought they had failed in their first great task. More than 3,000 Anzacs had been killed or wounded, and their beach-head was barely one-kilometre deep instead of seven. *'How we prayed for this ghastly day to end,'* one officer wrote.

When General Hamilton was awoken at midnight on board HMS *Queen Elizabeth* and given a message from Birdwood that the Anzacs might have to be evacuated, he replied firmly: 'Your news is serious indeed. But there is nothing for it but to dig yourselves in and stick it out. It would take at least two days to re-embark you … Dig, dig, dig, until you are safe.'

The British landings

None of the great hopes of the invasion had been achieved. In the south, at Cape Helles, British troops had landed from 6.30 a.m. in the morning of 25 April 1915 at half a dozen points. At some points they had met no resistance, at others they had been cut down in the surf by machine-gun fire. The Turkish defenders at Cape Helles numbered only 2,000 men, and by nightfall 20,000 British troops were ashore, but had advanced barely 1.7 kilometres inland. In the next eight months, as Turkish reinforcements poured in, the line was to barely move. On the first day of the Gallipoli campaign, stalemate had been reached.

The exact number of Anzac casualties is unknown, but they exceeded those of the British because 1,800 wounded men alone were evacuated from Anzac Cove in the first 24 hours. In the first five days at Anzac Cove, the casualties there totalled more than 8,000 killed and wounded, while British casualties at Cape Helles in the first seven days were 5,000.

AE2 breaks through

Hamilton then received the cheering news: 'An Australian submarine has done the finest feat in submarine history.' On 25 April 1915, the little sub AE2 had succeeded where many other attempts had failed. She battled swirling currents and scraped past mine cables to enter the Sea of Marmara where she quickly sank a Turkish gunboat. AE2 roamed there at will for five days before being disabled by a Turkish shell and scuttled. Happily, her English captain, Lieutenant-Commander Stoker, and most of his 30 Australian crew survived captivity. British submarines sank Turkish warships and transports over succeeding months: one of the few victories in the campaign.

Gallipoli and the Middle East, 1915–18

Gallipoli: 'Digging in'

The Australians on Gallipoli had already begun to dig and within a day all thought of evacuation was dismissed. Dawn broke on 26 April 1915 to an extraordinary sight at 'Anzac', which was soon the code-name for the Australian-occupied beach-head. The Australians were holding a line of ridges a kilometre inland from the coast and running about five kilometres from south to north, with the New Zealanders in the northern trenches. The Australians were fortifying two exposed posts only five metres from the Turks known as Quinn's Post and Courtney's Post (after the officers who had seized them). Their approaches were under Turkish sniper fire and reinforcements could only reach them under the cover of night.

Over the next few months the Anzacs dug trenches, 'pozzies' and tunnels so industriously that one Turkish officer wrote: *'These Australians will tunnel to Constantinople!'*

Water, water

The troops discovered early that there was not a drop of water at Anzac Cove. Fresh water had to be shipped to the beach in barrels and carried up to the trenches. Soon, an armada of small boats brought in supplies, food, ammunition and

The front line trenches at Gallipoli were under constant sniper fire. Note the Anzac soldier using a periscope rifle while his mates rest.

Australia in History

Simpson and his donkey

One Australian soldier at Anzac Cove was distressed by the agonies of the wounded and the lack of medical orderlies. When he found a stray donkey in a gully, he began using it to bring wounded soldiers from the front line down to the beach. He was a young 'Geordie' from north-east England who had enlisted in the AIF under the name Simpson, but his real name was John Simpson Kirkpatrick. Simpson and his donkey 'Murphy' became a familiar sight to the Anzacs over the next week. He was killed by a stray enemy bullet on 19 May 1915, four days after General Bridges had been killed by a sniper. Simpson lives on in legend as the Good Samaritan of Gallipoli.

reinforcements, and pontoons were built. Anzac Cove looked like a miniature harbour and was soon the home of 30,000 men.

The English war correspondent Ellis Ashmead-Bartlett, who had written a thrilling but highly coloured account of how the Australians had charged up steep cliffs to drive off the Turks, wrote: *'The Australians are in the most extraordinary position an army has ever found itself, clinging as they are to the face of a cliff.'* Colonel Monash of Melbourne wrote to his wife: *'To a stranger it would probably look like a disturbed ant heap, with everyone running a different way, but the whole thing is really a triumph of organisation.'* A British officer wrote: *'One met Australians all over the place, wandering around, drinking tea and having potshots at anything they saw.'* Other visitors to the extraordinary beach-head mention the din of bullets and shell-bursts. For the next eight months there would be hardly a moment of quiet. Sniping at the Turks became a form of sport. Australians invented the periscope rifle so that they could spot the enemy and fire without getting their heads shot off. Soon they were joking in the face of death.

By 1 May 1915, when Anzac casualties had reached more than 8,000, Hamilton asked the Anzacs to reinforce the British in the south. At Cape Helles, the Anzacs were delighted to see flat country covered with spring flowers. The poppies and daisies were soon stained by their blood, as an Anzac brigade was ordered to advance in daylight against the Turkish lines at Krithia. One thousand Victorian soldiers fell in minutes to point-blank machine-gun fire. They had never wavered.

The Battle of Anzac

At 3 a.m. on the morning of 19 May 1915, there were barely 17,000 Anzac troops at Anzac Cove, when they were attacked by an army of 42,000 Turks. The Anzacs, with their machine-guns well sited, stood their ground and cut down the enemy in thousands. At battle's end, 10,000 Turks had fallen and half of them lay dead and dying in 'No Man's Land'. Anzac casualties totalled only 628 men.

In the days following, as the cries of the wounded continued and the hot sun rose, the Anzacs were moved to pity. They had never seen such bravery before. A truce was arranged and Anzacs and Turks together helped to bury the dead. It is said that the Australians' hatred of the Turks died that day and was replaced by a healthy respect. From then on, the Turks were fellow sufferers; human beings.

The Turks never again attempted to dislodge the Anzacs. The troops were there to stay and they made the best of it, mocking their sad plight, enduring heat and thirst and wounds without too much complaint. Soon the navy disappeared from the waters of Gallipoli, and a terrible loneliness settled over the peninsula.

Gallipoli and the Middle East, 1915–18

Gallipoli: Stalemate

Battles in London

On 12 May 1915 tragedy had struck: the battleship HMS *Ocean* was torpedoed at Cape Helles and went down with 600 of her sailors. Alarmed that German submarines might sink the mighty battleship HMS *Queen Elizabeth* – the first of the oil-fired Dreadnoughts – the fiery Lord Fisher demanded that she be withdrawn from Gallipoli. Five days later, the Anzacs watched in horror as another battleship HMS *Triumph* was sunk by torpedo off the beaches; two days after that, enemy torpedoes claimed yet another, HMS *Majestic*.

With the coming of summer, the heat and lack of water became intense. The troops on Gallipoli were wasted by disease.

Australia in History

16

Lord Kitchener was preparing to send more troops to Gallipoli, yet Lord Fisher was now cancelling a new naval assault on the Straits and demanding the withdrawal of most of his battleships. Fisher now turned on Churchill, writing: *'You are bent on forcing the Dardanelles and nothing will turn you from it – nothing! I know you so well.'* He then resigned.

Britain's Prime Minister Asquith, attempting to form a **coalition** government with the Conservatives, was now faced with their demands that Winston Churchill be removed from office. When Churchill, the scapegoat for the expedition, was forced to resign from the Admiralty on 21 May 1915, any chance of obtaining full naval support in Gallipoli ended. The army was on its own.

It was not until early June 1915 that the Australian government released the names of the men killed and wounded to the newspapers – a list of nearly 10,000 names. But their families read also of how the Australians had fought gallantly in numerous battles. Instead of feelings of outrage at the disaster, they felt wild pride in the bravery of their men. *'Boys, you have honoured our land,'* wrote a young female Ballarat schoolteacher. The British had once described the Australians as the least likely men to make good soldiers, but were now calling them magnificent fighters – 'the best the world has seen'. Australians had never had great pride in their young nation, but they now felt a pride in their soldiers that would never diminish.

Gallipoli: The summer break-out

While the army stood marooned on Gallipoli, its strength sapped by disease, undernourishment and casualties, General Hamilton had a brainwave. He would land new armies and stage a massive offensive to break-out of the beach-heads. The idea came to him from Anzac Cove, where Birdwood reported that patrols had found no Turks in the land north of Anzac Cove. Another party of New Zealanders had probed even further north, and walked across the hard dry surface of the salt lake at Suvla Bay without sighting a Turk. Hamilton resolved to land a new army at Suvla while the Anzacs launched attacks on the Turkish line to distract them. The New Zealanders would capture the great height of Chunuk Bair and the undefended ground in the north, while the Australians stormed two of the most strongly-defended positions facing them – Lone Pine and the narrow ridge called 'The Nek'. As reinforcements were brought into Anzac Cove and Cape Helles under cover of night, the troops sensed that something big was about to happen, and their morale was high.

Lone Pine and The Nek

The great summer offensives were to begin late on 6 August 1915. When the Australians of 1st Brigade (NSW) filed into their trenches facing Lone Pine, the AIF 'official correspondent' noted that they were in good spirits and was struck by *'the qualities that never ceased to surprise even those who knew the Australian soldier best … There was not the slightest sign of nervousness in face, speech or action.'* At exactly 5.30 p.m., the instant the naval bombardment of the Turkish lines ceased, the whistles blew and the Australians rose from the trenches and charged across the open ground, jumping into the enemy lines and fighting their way through the crazy maze of trenches and dugouts. It was the most bloody fighting Australians had ever known, and it raged for three days, man against man. Men hurled hand-made bombs (grenades) or defended their trenches with bayonets when their bullets ran out. When Turkish counter-attacks ended three days later they had lost 10,000 men. The Australians had lost nearly 3,000 men and won seven **Victoria Crosses**.

In the afternoon of 9 August 1915, the Light Horse men facing the Turks at the narrow Nek charged forward again and again, cut to pieces by enemy machine-guns. When an officer pleaded that further attacks be halted he was over-ruled. The Australians were sent forward again to meet the same terrible fate. The tragedy forms the climax of the famous film *Gallipoli*.

Gallipoli and the Middle East, 1915–18

Gallipoli: The campaign fails

The New Zealanders

After nightfall on 6 August 1915, a column of New Zealanders had left their lines and stealthily advanced into the rugged terrain to their north. Eight hours later, as dawn was breaking, they stood on the slope leading to Chunuk Bair itself. They let out a mighty shout of triumph that floated over the gullies. By this brilliant deed the New Zealanders had tripled the size of the Anzac bridgehead in a matter of hours. But their reinforcement brigade was delayed and when the advance to the crest of Chunuk Bair began the Turks were waiting. The New Zealanders attacked the next day and then held the crest against massive counter-attacks before their survivors were relieved by British troops. But on 10 August a tidal wave of Turks wrestled back the crest of Chunuk Bair. Yet another assault column of Anzacs and Indian troops had become lost in the nightmare gullies of Aghyl Dere, and encountered violent Turkish counter-attacks. General Hamilton's great plan was coming apart.

Suvla Bay

Everything now hinged on Suvla Bay, where a vast British army had landed without opposition on the night of 6 August 1915. General Hamilton's staff officers discovered that the troops had not advanced from the beaches. The generals were befuddled, the junior British officers were inexperienced, and their men calmly waited for orders that never came. When the British troops at Suvla Bay advanced across the salt lake on 21 August, they marched into terrible Turkish artillery and machine-gun fire. On the first day 5,000 men fell. The advance stagnated.

The Murdoch letter

Meanwhile, Australian newspaper correspondent Keith Murdoch (the father of today's media billionaire Rupert Murdoch) had visited Gallipoli. He was appalled by the shambles and wrote a long report for the Australian Prime Minister. Murdoch wrote: *'If you could picture Anzac as I have seen it, you would find that to be an Australian is the greatest privilege the world has to offer …'* But he

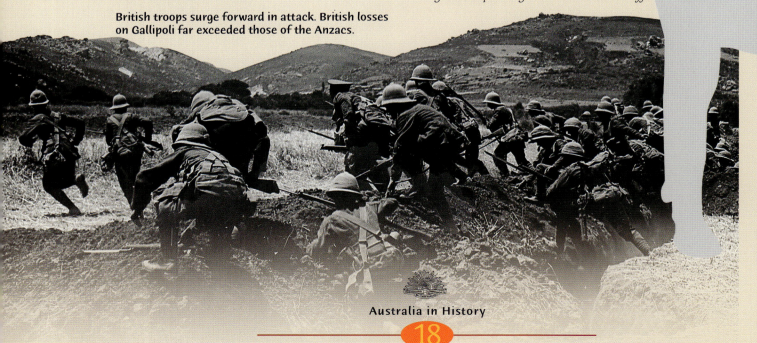

British troops surge forward in attack. British losses on Gallipoli far exceeded those of the Anzacs.

Australia in History

18

also added: *'The spirit at Suvla is simply deplorable.'* Murdoch made sure that copies were circulated to members of the British Cabinet.

In October 1915, General Hamilton was sacked as C-in-C and replaced by General Monro, who visited the Gallipoli peninsula and recommended that plans be made for evacuation.

Admitting defeat

Lord Kitchener also visited the peninsula in November. There he saw the conditions of the men he had sent to the gates of hell. On Gallipoli, an army of 134,000 men and 14,000 animals awaited the storms and snow of winter. The troops were unaware that the end was near. Just after Kitchener's visit, Brigadier-General Monash wrote to his wife from his dug-out: *'I can hear machine-guns and rifles going like mad … The Turks are real sports, and men in the front trenches often play off jokes on each other, such as putting up dummies to be fired at, or pretending to charge … '*

Adding to the misery, winter storms began and snows fell on the trenches. Men now stood in mud, winds howled, and storms swept away the jetties at Anzac Cove. On 2 November 1915, it was finally decided to evacuate the army.

The evacuation begins

The problem now was how to take the troops off Gallipoli without the Turks noticing. It was thought that half the men would be lost during the evacuation. The Turks were tricked into believing that the Allied troops were digging in for winter. From the night of 11 December, the men were led down to the beaches, unit by unit. Some soldiers continued to man the forward trenches. When they too departed, rifles were rigged up to keep firing automatically to give the impression that men were still in the trenches. By 19 December 1915, 50,000 men at Anzac Cove had been taken off by the navy without a single fatality, as were the 40,000 men at Suvla. It was the one triumph of the campaign.

Gallipoli remembered

The Gallipoli campaign had ended sadly in defeat. Allied casualties totalled 250,000. Of these, nearly 50,000 men were killed or died of their wounds or disease. Among the dead were 10,100 Anzacs (7,600 Australians and 2,500 New Zealanders). Turkish losses were equally horrifying – more than 250,000 men. At least 23 Turkish divisions had fought on Gallipoli and they never recovered from their losses. Soon Gallipoli was submerged by all the other great campaigns of the First World War. *'But Anzac stood, and still stands,'* wrote the Australian Official Historian, *'for reckless valour in a good cause, for enterprise, resourcefulness, fidelity, comradeship and endurance that will never know defeat.'*

The Anzacs had never given up. They left Gallipoli without hatred in their heart for their enemy or bitterness at the incompetence of their own high command. The anniversary of the landing – 25 April – has ever since been a day of remembrance in Australia and New Zealand, whose people felt pride that their men had been acclaimed as heroes. Every year, young Australians visit the Gallipoli peninsula to pay tribute to the heroic soldiers who died there so far from their homeland.

The New Zealanders won an acclaim equal to the Australians on Gallipoli. These young New Zealanders are on convalescent leave.

Gallipoli and the Middle East, 1915–18

Egypt, Iraq and oil

Defending Egypt, 1916

Early in 1916 the vast army evacuated from Gallipoli and the garrison in Egypt totalled 250,000 men – an army of 10 divisions. The streets of Cairo and Alexandria bustled with thousands of soldiers on leave – English and Scots, Anzacs and French. But within two months most of the French and British infantry, including the Australians, were hastily shipped to France and the Western Front, where the Germans had just launched a massive offensive on Verdun.

The desert

In the Middle East, the summer temperatures – particularly in July and August – are scorching. They sometimes reach 51°Celsius in the shade, but there is little shade in the desert. The horizon shimmers in the heat, and armies learned to move in the cool of night, finding their way by the stars. Though much of the desert terrain is hard – like gravel – the sand dunes of the Sinai Desert are endless. In summer, the desert wells dry up and water is scarce. It is literally too hot to fight. From March to May the desert is whipped by sandstorms blown by hot winds – the *khamsin* – that can blot out visibility for days on end.

The British formed a Camel Corps to traverse the desert with supplies. Some learnt to enjoy riding camels, while others were sentenced to serve in the Camel Corps for punishment.

Australia in History

The Light Horse

Soon, only four weakened British second-line infantry divisions remained to garrison Egypt, the base for future operations in the Middle East. Yet the Anzac horsemen were to fight in the desert for the remainder of the war. The three Australian Light Horse Brigades and the New Zealand Mounted Brigade were formed into the 'Anzac Mounted Division' under the command of Major-General Harry Chauvel, a 51-year-old Queensland officer. They formed the largest force of Anzac horsemen that had ever been assembled. By March 1916, as the hot weather began, they thought they were in for a dull year of patrols, with no threat from the Turks until summer ended.

Disaster in Mesopotamia (Iraq)

In November 1914, British-Indian forces landed in the Persian Gulf to secure the oil pipeline and Abadan refinery, and then occupied Basra. In April 1915, they began advancing north into Iraq to pacify the tribes, and then made the mistake of advancing even further up the Tigris River to seize Baghdad. In December 1915, they were stopped by a strong Turkish army only 20 kilometres from Baghdad and forced to retreat to Kut. There, in April 1916, General Townshend's army grew weak when their food was exhausted and he was forced to surrender. Of Townshend's 13,000 men, barely 3,000 survived captivity. Another 23,000 British and Indian soldiers had been lost in attempting to relieve him. It was the greatest humiliation the British Army had suffered for a century.

Australian airmen had served in Iraq from early 1915. Four pilots arrived (accompanied by 40 mechanics or ground crew) to fly the primitive planes there. They soon proved their worth flying over the desert to spot enemy troop movements, but all were killed or captured by tribesmen. In December 1916, General Maude, commanding a reinforced British army, advanced from Basra in the cool of winter, entering in March 1917.

Oil

The man described as 'the founder of the Middle East oil industry' was an Australian millionaire named William Knox D'Arcy. Looking for fresh investments, D'Arcy felt that oil might be found south of the Caucasus and obtained a concession from the Persian Shah. His drillers discovered oil after a seven-year search in 1908, and D'Arcy then built a pipeline from the derricks to a huge refinery at Abadan on the Persian Gulf. In June 1914, the British government bought a majority shareholding in D'Arcy's Anglo-Persian Oil Company (later known as British Petroleum, or BP) to ensure an oil supply for the Royal Navy. It proved to be the most profitable investment the British government ever made.

The Australian Light Horse were mounted infantrymen, but they excelled as scouts. In the famous Battle of Beersheba, they charged the enemy on horseback.

Gallipoli and the Middle East, 1915–18

From Egypt to Palestine

In March 1916, the Commander-in-Chief in Cairo, General Murray, was astonished to hear that the enemy was advancing from Palestine towards the Suez Canal in a second attempt to seize it. In April, the Turks overwhelmed the English outposts in the Sinai, and small Light Horse patrols rode out to seal the wells in their way. Aircraft reported that the Turks seemed to be heading for Romani, near the coast. Murray decided to tempt the Turks into attacking Romani where his mobile force, the Anzac Mounted Division, could fall on the enemy flanks. Murray's 10,000 men were facing 14,000 Turks. The seesaw battle began under the stars in the early hours of 2 August 1916 and lasted through five days of close fighting in terrible heat. The Turks, exhausted, finally retreated, having lost nearly 5,000 men killed and wounded and 5,000 captured. British casualties were 1,130 men, nearly all of them Anzacs. Romani was a stunning victory and proved the remarkable qualities of the Anzacs and of their horses.

The Desert Column

In December 1916, the 'Desert Column' – as the Anzac mounted troops were now known – led the army into El Arish, which the Turks had evacuated. The newly arrived No. 1 Squadron, Australian Flying Corps, played an important part in observing Turkish movements. The Anzac Mounted was now reinforced by a new brigade named the Imperial Camel Corps (mainly made up of Anzacs). Capturing the inland village of Magdhaba, the Anzacs advanced a fortnight later on Rafa, which they took after heavy fighting.

The sand dunes of the Sinai were behind the Anzacs and they now rode through fields of waving grass. They were on the threshold of Palestine. As his troops advanced, General Murray had laid down a railway and a pipeline to keep the forces supplied.

Below: Turkish prisoners under British guard in Cairo.

The Arab revolt

When the Muslim Turkish Sultan proclaimed a *jihad* (Holy War) against the 'infidels', the British mistakenly thought that the Emir Husain of the Hejaz, Grand Sherif of Mecca, could become an ally and a figure of equal prestige in the Arab world. Late in 1914, Lord Kitchener assured Husain that if the Arabs threw off Turkish rule, Britain would recognize their independence. Soon afterwards, the Sherif expressed his desire to become ruler of the entire Arab world after the defeat of Turkey – this was a development the Allies had not foreseen.

In the meantime, the British and French planned the fate of Turkey's empire. The resulting 'Sykes-Picot Agreement' of 1916 outlined a division of the Turkish Empire into British, French and Russian spheres. The heart of the Holy Land, the city of Jerusalem (where a small Jewish community had existed for thousands of years), would be a tiny enclave under international control. Britain would gain oil-rich Mesopotamia (modern Iraq), while 'Palestine', the vast stretch of land connecting Iraq to the Mediterranean, would form an Arab kingdom for Husain under British protection. France would have control of the Syrian coastline including Lebanon, and influence in Syria's interior, while Russia gained Kurdistan and parts of Anatolia.

The secret agreement later proved totally unworkable. Husain, who knew nothing of it, remained uncommitted to the Allies until he heard that a Turkish force was marching to arrest him. On 5 June 1916, Husain raised the standard of revolt in Mecca. British officers were depressed to find that Husain's army amounted to only 3,000 tribesmen. It would take a year before figures like Colonel T.E. Lawrence – 'Lawrence of Arabia' – could turn them into an effective guerrilla army.

Colonel T.E. Lawrence was the most successful British officer in winning the trust of the Arabs. 'Lawrence of Arabia' helped to form Husain's Arabs into an effective army.

Promises to the Jews

To confuse matters, Britain promised to create a 'home' for the world's Jews in Palestine. The British government had long been the only Great Power to show sympathy for the sad plight of the Jewish people whose communities were scattered across the world. In November 1917, Lord Balfour, Britain's Foreign Secretary, declared that 'His Majesty's Government view with favour the establishment in Palestine of a national home for the Jewish people … it being clearly understood that nothing shall be done which may prejudice the civil and religious rights of existing non-Jewish communities in Palestine.'

Gallipoli and the Middle East, 1915–18

Advancing to Jerusalem

Blocking the way to Palestine along the coast was the town of Gaza. Australian pilots venturing over it in their slow two-seaters found it thick with anti-aircraft guns and German fighters. When an Australian pilot was forced down in the desert near a Turkish camp, a comrade, who was already wounded, landed next to his plane to rescue him. They took off amid a hail of bullets, pursued by horsemen and made it 120 kilometres back to base. The rescuer, Frank MacNamara, was awarded the AFC's first Victoria Cross.

The battles for Gaza

One night at the end of March 1917, the Anzac Mounted Division rode out to take up positions north of Gaza. The British infantry attacks on the town from the south were beaten back with heavy loss and the battle was called off. In mid-April, the British made another attack on Gaza which also failed to break the defences. General Murray's two attacks had cost 10,000 casualties. He unwisely described the second attack as a successful operation because enemy losses had also been heavy. In June 1917, Murray was replaced by a new Commander-in-Chief, General Sir Edmund Allenby, who had commanded an army in France.

Allenby takes command

Allenby was a big, impressive man with a hot temper who often frightened his own officers. But 'The Bull', as he was called, was also intelligent. He often visited front-line troops, arriving on horseback in a cloud of dust, interrogating officers and sacking them on the spot if he found them inefficient and unable to answer his questions. General Chauvel, now appointed to command the 'Desert Mounted Corps' stood up to Allenby and grew to admire him.

Allenby's generals drew up plans to bypass the Turkish front line which ran from the coast at

Australian Light Horse men are shown taking up defensive positions prior to battle.

Australia in History

Gaza to the village and oasis of Beersheba. They would capture Beersheba and take Gaza from the rear. By brilliant subterfuge, Allenby lulled the Turks into thinking the sole attack would fall on Gaza alone.

The charge at Beersheba

On 31 October 1917, the British guns opened up and infantry assaults began on Gaza. The infantry had to fight their way over open desert and through barbed wire and machine-gun fire in full view of the defenders. By late afternoon little progress had been made. General Chauvel and his Anzac horsemen had already taken their positions south-east of Beersheba. There, Chauvel noticed from aerial photos that no deep ditches or barbed wire defended Beersheba on his section of the front. At 3.30 p.m. he decided to launch his last reserve, the 4th Light Horse Brigade, in a headlong attack across the seven kilometres of open ground to capture the town and its fresh-water wells before darkness fell.

The Light Horse Brigade charged forward at dusk, taking the Turks by surprise. Within minutes, the Light Horse had jumped the enemy trenches and galloped into the centre of Beersheba where they captured the vital wells before the enemy could detonate them. For the loss of 67 casualties, they had won a brilliant victory. Gaza was now outflanked. One week later, Gaza fell and the road to Jerusalem was open. But the British advance pushed north up the coast leaving Jerusalem far to their south-east because Allenby was concentrating on encircling the retreating Turks. When the winter rains came, however, all operations bogged down in the mud. After skirmishes, the Holy City was evacuated by the Turks. On 12 December 1917, Allenby entered Jerusalem to the cheers of the Christian and Jewish population.

Across the Jordan

In February 1918, Allenby sent his forces into the lifeless terrain of the Jordan Valley east of Jerusalem, intending to seize Amman (now the capital of Jordan). His troops would have to seize Jericho near the Dead Sea which lay nearly half a kilometre below sea level, before fighting their way up the mountains to Amman.

The Anzac Mounted Division reached Es Salt and moved up towards Amman, but its defences were strong. The isolated troops withdrew in a snowstorm. In April 1918, Allenby's Anzacs and British troops were forced back. As summer wore on, the Jordan Valley became hotter than a furnace. Allenby waited until the worst of summer's heat ended.

Lieut-General Chauvel visits the Australian Flying Corps' first squadron. He is seen standing to the left of its commanding officer Major Richard Williams (holding cane), the future 'Father of the RAAF'.

Gallipoli and the Middle East, 1915–18

Syria: Galloping to victory

The Turkish armies, though numbering 100,000 men, were now exhausted, short of supplies and in low morale. Allenby's armies now numbered 140,000 (but only half of them were front-line troops). They were well-supplied and he had complete control of the air. Allenby decided to attack before winter came, in September 1918, on the coastal plain at Megiddo – the Armageddon of the Bible. If he could break the strong enemy front, Allenby would let the Desert Mounted Corps ride north as far as their horses and supplies would carry them – to Anatolia itself.

Megiddo to Damascus

The Turks were bluffed into believing Allenby's main attack would be mounted on the eastern end of his line. But his offensive would fall in the west, on the coastal sector. The Turks transferred entire divisions from the west to the east, waiting for an attack that never came. Soon only 8,000 Turks were manning the line in the west and they were faced by 40,000 British and Anzac troops. Allenby ordered the air force to bomb Turkish telephone exchanges and asked Lawrence's Arabs to blow up the Damascus-Hejaz rail lines behind the enemy front so that no reinforcements could reach the Turks.

On 19 September 1918, Allenby's artillery and infantry attacked at Megiddo, and four hours later his Desert Mounted Corps went forward through the gap they had made. The battle had gone exactly to plan. Within two days, the Australians had ridden as far as Samaria and the Turkish armies were in retreat, being harassed constantly from the air. On 25 September, the Anzac Mounted Division swung east and rode into Amman. The Division took 10,300 prisoners, and lost only 139 men. Allenby ordered the rest of Chauvel's Anzacs to press north to Beirut and Damascus.

Damascus

On 1 October 1918, the Australian Light Horse entered the ancient city of Damascus. They had originally intended to bypass it, but were so exhausted that they were falling asleep in the saddle, and they took the historic short cut. They beat Lawrence's Arabs to Damascus by three days, but the British decided it was diplomatic to tell the world that Husain's son Faisal had liberated Damascus. Chauvel soon made sure the truth was known.

By 26 October, the Desert Mounted Corps had reached Aleppo in northern Syria. But here the advance ended because Turkey had asked for an **armistice**. Allenby told Chauvel that his men had ridden 'in the greatest cavalry feat the world has ever known.'

Since the September offensive began, the Australians had taken more than 30,000 prisoners and had lost only 93 men killed or wounded. In the terrible bloodbath of the First World War, the Middle East campaigns were the only ones where the generals used brains instead of brawn.

Left: General Sir Edmund Allenby (later Field-Marshal Lord Allenby) was sent to Egypt as a form of demotion. However, in the Middle East he proved to be a commander of genius.

Australia in History

The armistice

Four days before Allenby's great offensive had begun, the Allied armies at Salonika had launched their own offensive against Bulgaria. Bulgaria, already exhausted by three years of war, signed a cease-fire (26 September 1918) and Austria-Hungary, menaced by an Italian offensive, signed an armistice on 1 November. Germany followed on 11 November.

Soon the Australians and New Zealanders would return in troopships to their homes and their families. Because of quarantine restrictions, their horses were not allowed to return. To many Anzacs this was the saddest parting of all.

Islam and its sects

Soon the victorious European powers would have to deal with the world of Islam, worshippers of a faith that stretches from north Africa through the Arab Middle East to central Asia and the islands of Indonesia. Islam has many sects, some of them extreme in their interpretation of their holy writings, which are largely based on the Koran (Qu'ran). Most Muslims belong to the Sunni faith and are violently opposed by the fervent faith known as Shia (Shi'ite). The Wahhabi sect dominant in Saudi Arabia is more **fundamentalist** even than the Shi'ites.

One British official in 1914 attempted to explain the three major sects by likening the Sunni to Protestantism, the Shia to Roman Catholicism (a more moralistic and demanding faith than Protestantism) and the Wahhabi to extreme Puritanism. But there is no simple explanation of any religion. Many European and American leaders, ignorant of Arab and Islamic beliefs and customs, were destined to make disastrous errors of judgement in their dealings with these cultures well into the present time.

Among the prisoners taken in the last Middle East offensives were numbers of Germans. Photograph taken at Es Salt in 1918.

Gallipoli and the Middle East, 1915–18

The Middle East: Picking up the pieces

The First World War was officially over. But converting the armistices into formal peace treaties would be a long and difficult task. In mid-November 1918, an Allied fleet dropped anchor at Constantinople and the Sultan awaited orders from the Allied high command. The Turkish Empire had ceased to exist. British and Indian troops now garrisoned its wide domains. But within months the Middle East was in chaos. The unrest began in Egypt, which had always been one of the most stable countries under British rule. In November 1918, only two days after the war with Germany had ended, a delegation of Nationalist leaders asked the British High Commissioner to end **martial** law and allow Egyptians to attend the Paris Peace Conference. When the British refused, rioting broke out and soon spread throughout Egypt. To restore order in Egypt, Allenby was recalled to Cairo and the Australian Light Horse regiments were ordered to patrol the streets. Allenby freed the imprisoned leader Zaghul and promised Egypt a return to parliamentary rule, which was accomplished in 1922.

India was also wracked by unrest. In April 1919, troops had opened fire on an 'illegal gathering' in the Sikh city of Amritsar, killing hundreds of people. The British 'raj' was no longer seen as protector of the Indian masses but as oppressor. A month later, tribesmen from Afghanistan invaded India; they were defeated but Britain had to give up its right to dictate Afghanistan's foreign policy. At the height of its imperial power, Britain was now faced with new and rising forces of **nationalism**.

A British general (centre) takes the surrender of Kuneitra, 28 September 1918. The figure on the right is Brigadier-General William Grant, the Victorian grazier who led the Light Horse at the Battle of Beersheba.

Australia in History

28

Carving up Turkey

In May 1919, the carve-up of Turkey began. Britain and France had promised Greece and Italy part of Turkish Anatolia. Lawlessness in towns on the Black Sea forced the Sultan to dispatch his best general, Kemal, to restore order there. When Greek forces began landing on the Aegean coast, Kemal formed an army to expel them, beginning a war between Greeks and Turks that lasted two years. By August 1920, the Greek Army had almost reached Angora and the Sultan's weak government was forced to sign the peace treaty at Sévres that handed over much of the Aegean coast and islands to the Greeks. Armenia was to become independent and Kurdistan autonomous. The treaty outraged patriotic Turks, and Kemal renounced the Sultan's authority and led an army to expel the invaders.

Syria created

The war's end had found Husain's son Faisal established in Damascus where he proclaimed himself King of Syria. In July 1920, French armies in Beirut, concerned at the Syrians' growing ties with Kemal's Turks, marched on Damascus and expelled Faisal, who sought refuge in British Palestine. The French proclaimed a protectorate over Syria and 'Greater Lebanon' which they enlarged from the coastal city of Beirut, home of Maronite Christians, to include a large number of Muslims, thus laying the foundations for a small, fractured and artificial nation.

In Palestine, the Arabs rose up against the small Jewish population in 1920. In Mesopotamia (Iraq), tribal uprisings against the British continued. Late in the year, Winston Churchill, back in government as Colonial Secretary, realized that Britain's Middle East policies had managed to upset everyone, and that a solution must be found.

Mesopotamia becomes Iraq

In March 1921, Churchill called a great conference in Cairo. There he decided that Mesopotamia would form a new kingdom called Iraq, ruled by the refugee from Syria, Prince Faisal. The previously separate Turkish provinces of Basra (Shi'ite), Baghdad (Sunni) and Kirkuk-Mosul (home of the Kurds) were united under the rule of an Arabian prince. Iraq was the most unstable of all the new creations – the king's young grandson, Faisal II, was murdered in a military coup in 1958. The oil-rich country soon fell under the cruel tyranny of Saddam Hussein, whose power was broken in 2003 by the armed forces of the United States, Britain and Australia.

Transjordan created

Palestine, Churchill decided, would be divided at the Jordan River, the land west of it forming the 'Mandate of Palestine' where Jews and Arabs would hopefully live side by side. The desert region east of the Jordan would form the Emirate of Transjordan, ruled by Faisal's brother Abdullah and supported by large British subsidies.

Persia becomes Iran

In Persia, where the Shah's rule was almost non-existent, the leader of his bodyguard, Reza Pahlevi, rode into Teheran in February 1921, with British encouragement, and declared himself Commander-in-Chief. Two weeks later, he rejected the new Anglo-Persian Agreement. Three years later, Pahlevi forced the Shah into exile and declared himself Shah. He attempted, like Kemal, to Westernise his people. Pahlevi changed Persia's name to Iran (a reminder of its Aryan origins) but angered the Shi'ite mullahs by his ruthless attempts to reduce their power. His dynasty's rule lasted until 1979.

Gallipoli and the Middle East, 1915–18

The making of the modern Middle East

Modern Turkey

Meanwhile, the Turkish-Greek war was marching to its climax. In August 1922, the Turks turned back the Greek Army near Angora and pursued it to Smyrna, which was put to the torch. Kemal then marched his army to the Dardanelles, where he faced a small British occupation force. When Lloyd George appealed for military assistance from the Dominions to defend the Dardanelles, only New Zealand promised troops. A second Gallipoli campaign was narrowly averted. The British withdrew and Kemal marched into Constantinople. The Sultan was forced to abdicate. By the end of 1922, both Lloyd George and Winston Churchill had lost office. It seemed that both men had reached the end of their turbulent political careers.

Kemal Atatürk, the first President of the Turkish Republic.

Kemal proclaimed the Turkish Republic and signed a new peace treaty with the Allies in 1923 at Lausanne in Switzerland. It guaranteed his existing frontiers and returned the Dardanelles to Turkey. The idea of separate states of Armenia and Kurdistan died.

Over the next 15 years of his life, Kemal almost completely modernised Turkey. Regarding religion as superstition, he abolished religious courts, adopted the Swiss Civil Code to give women equality with men, and forbade the wearing of traditional Islamic head-dress and clothing. He replaced Arabic with the Roman alphabet and forced his people to adopt surnames; Kemal renamed Constantinople 'Istanbul' and adopted the surname Atatürk ('Father of the Turks'). In 1936, Turkey was granted *total* control of the Dardanelles. When Kemal Atatürk died in 1938, he was both feared and revered.

Turkey continued Kemal's policies of development and avoidance of ruinous wars. Though neutral, she remained pro-Allied throughout the course of the Second World War of 1939–45. Young Australians and New Zealanders who visit the Gallipoli peninsula find the graves of the Anzacs there maintained with care and respect by their former enemies.

Saudi Arabia and oil

Husain, King of the Hejaz, had the satisfaction of seeing two of his sons on the thrones of the new nations of Transjordan (today's Jordan) and Iraq. But Husain lost his own throne in 1924, when his old enemy Ibn Saud conquered the Hejaz and declared himself ruler of 'Saudi Arabia'. Saud's huge kingdom was near bankrupt, relying for

Australia in History

30

income on dried fruits, banditry and the pilgrims visiting Mecca. The desert kingdoms were transformed by the discovery of oil. In 1927, oil was found at Kirkuk in northern Iraq and at Bahrein in 1932. In 1938, massive oil fields were then found in Kuwait and Saudi Arabia. American and British oil companies divided the Arab world into spheres of influence – the Americans enjoyed dominance in Saudi Arabia while the British companies dominated Iraq.

... And Palestine

Palestine, west of the Jordan, flourished as Jewish immigrants poured in during the 1920s and 1930s. They cultivated the barren ground, irrigated the desert, built settlements and towns. By 1936, the Jewish population had risen from 40,000 to 400,000. The Arabs were now outnumbered, but the foundations of today's strong State of Israel had been laid.

In 1936, the Arabs rebelled against the British and the Jewish settlers. In 1939, Britain prohibited further Jewish immigration to appease the Arabs. For millions of European Jews there was now no refuge from Nazi brutality. Soon, Muslim opposition towards Jews would grow into an unforgiving hatred. In creating nation states where none had previously existed, the Great Powers had laid the foundation of future disputes.

The aftermath

Thus was made the Middle East that we see today – a region of great antiquity transformed by wars, political rivalries and extraordinary economic growth, but made unstable by bitter nationalism and religious divisions.

In the Second World War of 1939–45, the Middle East again became the scene of great campaigns, and naval battles were fought in the Mediterranean. Australians again fought in the defence of Egypt and in campaigns from Libya to Syria, and in 1991 and 2003 served in wars against the ruthless Iraqi dictator, Saddam Hussein, that brought about his fall.

Emir Feisal and his staff at the Paris Peace Conference in 1919. Behind his left shoulder is Colonel T.E. Lawrence.

Gallipoli and the Middle East, 1915–18

Glossary

abdicate — to be forced to give up a throne
armistice — cease-fire (usually followed by a peace treaty)
artillery — heavy guns
autonomy — self-government within a nation
coalition — combination of nations
Dominions — self-governing nations in the British Empire
fundamentalist — basic, narrow religious belief
garrison — army base or fortress
Great Powers — the major nations of Europe
infantry — foot soldiers
martial — military
munitions — shells, bullets and bombs
mutiny — rebellion of an army
nationalism — desire of a people for self-rule or independence
neutral — uncommitted to any side
offensive — a planned, massed attack
protectorate — form of occupation of another country
stalemate — deadlock
Victoria Cross — the British Commonwealth's highest award for bravery in war

Index

AIF   6, 7, 15, 17
Allenby, General Sir Edmund   24, 25, 26, 27, 28
Anzac Cove   11, 12, 13, 14, 15, 17, 19
Anzacs   8, 9, 10, 11, 12, 13, 14, 15, 16, 17, 18, 19, 20, 22, 23, 24, 25, 26, 27, 30
Atatürk, Kemal   7, 12, 29, 30

Birdwood, Lieutenant General Sir William   8, 9, 11, 13
British Empire   6

Chauvel, Major-General Harry   21, 24, 25, 26
Churchill, Winston   9, 10, 17, 29
Constantinople   4, 5, 7, 9, 10, 14, 28, 30

Darnadelles   4, 5, 8, 9, 17, 30

Egypt   6, 7, 8, 9, 10, 20, 21, 22, 28, 29, 30, 31

Gallipoli   4, 5, 6, 8, 9, 10, 11, 12, 13, 14, 15, 16, 17, 18, 19, 20, 30
Great Powers   5, 7, 31

Hamilton, General Sir Ian   10, 11, 13, 15, 17, 18, 19

Lawrence, Colonel T.E. (Lawrence of Arabia)   23, 26, 31

Mesopotamia (Iraq)   7, 21, 23, 29, 31
Monash, Brigadier-General John   15, 19

oil   7, 21, 23, 29, 30, 31

Palestine   22, 23, 24, 29, 31
Pasha, Enver   7

Simpson and his donkey   15

Victoria Cross   17, 24

Australia in History